Brilliant BOATS

To Ann-Janine, Caroline and Suzanne – with thanks from Tony.
For Mister Mush and Scampy – A.P.

The Publisher thanks the National Maritime Museum, Greenwich for
their kind assistance in the development of this book.

First published 2002 by Kingfisher
This edition published 2013 by Macmillan Children's Books
an imprint of Pan Macmillan, a division of
Macmillan Publishers International Limited
20 New Wharf Road, London N1 9RR
Associated companies throughout the world
www.panmacmillan.com

ISBN: 978-1-4472-1263-8

Text copyright © Tony Mitton 2002
Illustrations copyright © Ant Parker 2002
Moral rights asserted.

5 7 9 8 6

A CIP catalogue record for this book is available from the British Library.

Printed in China

Brilliant
BOATS

Tony Mitton and
Ant Parker

MACMILLAN CHILDREN'S BOOKS

Boats are really brilliant for sailing us around.
They travel through the water
with a sloppy-slappy sound.

It's fun to go out boating, especially in the sun.
The water's cool and sparkly,
so come on everyone!

A boat sits on the water
like an empty bowl or cup.
It's hollow and it's full of air,
and that's what keeps it up.

An anchor holds you steady
when you're bobbing in a bay.
You wind a chain to raise it
when you want to sail away.

Over lakes and seas and rivers,
wind blows very strong.
Some boats have sails to catch it,
so it pushes them along.

To manage boats with masts and sails,
you need a clever crew.
The captain is the one in charge,
who tells them what to do.

A dinghy or a rowing boat
is useful near the shore.

You make it travel backwards
by pulling on each oar.

Capta

Whoosh!

A motor boat is powered
by propeller from the back.
It whooshes through the water
and leaves a foamy track.

And just in case, by accident,
you tumble from the boat,
you have to wear a life jacket,
made to help you float.

Some boats go out fishing
where the ocean waves are steep.

Their nets are cast to catch the fish,
then haul them from the deep.

A ship can carry cargo,
which is loaded at the docks.

Hup! Ho! Look out below!
Here comes a giant box.

A ferry carries cars and lorries
where they need to go.

The people travel up above.
The vehicles stay below.

A mighty ocean liner
has a big and busy crew.
It carries many passengers.
They're waving now. Yoo-hoo!

The ship has cosy cabins
where the passengers can stay.
And out on deck they stroll about
and watch the sea, or play.

But when the journey's over –
Ahoy! The lighthouse rock!

The ship glides into harbour
and ties up at the dock.

Boat bits

lighthouse

this is a tall building on the coast with a flashing light to guide ships and keep them away from rocks

anchor

this is a very heavy piece of metal with hooks which dig into the ground under the water to stop the boat drifting away

propeller

this has **blades** which spin round very fast at the back of the boat and push against the water to move the boat forward

oars

these are long poles with flat **blades** at the end which push against the water to move the boat forward

deck

this is the floor of a boat

cabin

this is the little room where you sleep on board a boat

cargo

this is the name for the goods that a ship transports

name

many boats are given names by their owners